Original title:
Rhymes Beneath the Canopy

Copyright © 2025 Creative Arts Management OÜ
All rights reserved.

Author: Christian Leclair
ISBN HARDBACK: 978-1-80567-199-2
ISBN PAPERBACK: 978-1-80567-498-6

Melodies in the Moss

In the woods where shadows creep,
Bugs do the tango, never sleep.
Mice wear hats, oh what a sight,
Dancing with owls in the moonlight.

Frogs flip-flop on lily pads,
Counting stars, ignoring their dads.
Beetles tap their tiny feet,
Singing songs that are quite offbeat.

Understory Dreams and Delights

Squirrels juggle acorns with flair,
Raccoons in tuxedos, quite the pair.
The trees gossip with vines up high,
While crickets chirp a lullaby.

Bunnies munch on candyfloss leaves,
Making wishes, pulling their sleeves.
Fireflies wink like little stars,
While ants ride bikes with tiny bars.

Fleeting Chants of the Wild

A parrot sings tunes from the charts,
While chipmunks paint with colorful arts.
The brook giggles, splashes, and plays,
Echoing laughter through sunny rays.

In laughter's embrace, the critters unite,
Drawing doodles in the soft moonlight.
Squirrels compete for the funniest show,
With weird flips that make everyone glow.

Hushed Harmonies in the Grove

The wind whispers secrets to trees so green,
Telling tales of the silliest scene.
Where raccoons wear shoes two sizes too big,
And frogs in bowties put on a jig.

Dancing shadows waltz with the night,
While owls hoot jokes that take flight.
A sense of mirth fills the cozy space,
In this quirky, enchanted place.

Ethereal Echoes of the Glen

In a glen where whispers sing,
Squirrels dance on a twig's spring,
They tell jokes to the trees,
As the leaves giggle in the breeze.

A rabbit tumbled, what a sight!
With hiccups that took flight,
The fox rolled back with glee,
As the mushrooms laughed in spree.

Murmurs in the Mossy Haven

In the moss, a party's spry,
Beetles wear a tie and fly,
They toast to the sugary dew,
As the mushrooms groove and chew.

A snail slips in with a glide,
Claiming he's the mossy guide,
But all the roaches burst in cheer,
Saying, "You're late, my dear!"

The Language of the Land Above

Above the ground, a chatter loud,
Starlings form a silly crowd,
The clouds poke fun, just out of reach,
While the sun teaches warmth its speech.

A branch broke free and made a fuss,
Claiming it was still on the bus,
The wind just chuckled, rather wise,
Saying, "You're just a branch in disguise!"

Treetops in Tune with the Twilight

When twilight paints the sky so bright,
The tree frogs start their karaoke night,
With poor pitch but joyful hearts,
They sing of love and old tree barks.

A raccoon drums on a tin can,
While a bear tries to catch a fan,
A bobcat joins, pretends to cheer,
And the moon just giggles, oh so near.

Verse of the Verdant Vault

In the forest where squirrels play,
A rabbit hops, and shouts hooray!
With acorns flying through the air,
The laughter rings, without a care.

A wise old owl wears glasses round,
He thinks he's king, though he's tree-bound.
The rabbits giggle, the foxes prance,
In this green world, they love to dance.

Woodland Wonders Unveiled

A woodpecker's tap is quite a beat,
He tries to dance with two left feet.
The deer just chuckles, says with glee,
"Join me, friend, let's sip some tea!"

A spider spins a silly web,
Inviting all for a funny ebb.
A frog croaks out a croaky tune,
While mushrooms sing beneath the moon.

Stanzas in the Sunlight Dappled

Under leaves, the sunlight peeks,
The chipmunks tease and play hide-and-seek.
A turtle dreams, all safe and slow,
While a breeze whispers a funny show.

The flowers wear hats, a colorful sight,
Swaying side to side, oh what a delight!
A butterfly flutters with flair and style,
While a grumpy old snail cracks a smile.

The Treetops' Timeless Tales

In the treetops, laughter echoes wide,
A raccoon jokes, with friends by his side.
"Why did the owl sit on a log?"
"To look like a wise and witty fog!"

The breeze tells tales of capers past,
Of mischief and fun that forever last.
A hedgehog giggles, rolls in the grass,
As every joke makes the woodland pass.

Lyrics in the Lattice of Branches

In the canopy, squirrels conspire,
Chasing their tails on a tightrope wire.
With acorn helmets and tiny boots,
They giggle and dance in their fuzzy suits.

A bird sings loud, and a rabbit hops,
Flopping around, while the forest drops.
A snail with shades takes a slow-motion slide,
As the critters cheer, with eyes open wide.

Enchanted Echoes of the Thicket

Down in the thicket, a frog plays the flute,
While a hedgehog jigs in a pin-cushion suit.
The mushrooms bob like they're in a trance,
As the fireflies join for a late-night dance.

A turtle twirls in a slow, funky beat,
While ants bring his snacks for the late-night treat.
With laughter that echoes through branches and leaves,
They form a band that the whole forest believes.

The Underbrush's Gentle Whispers

In the underbrush, secrets unfold,
As a raccoon tells tales, a bit too bold.
With a chipmunk's giggle and a badger's grin,
They plan a parade as the sun dips in.

A hedgehog rides, on a snail's back too,
Dressed in a cape made of morning dew.
The leaves rustle soft, as they jest and tease,
In their leafy realm, where they do as they please.

Forest's Ballad: A Hidden Harmony

Amidst the trees, a party's begun,
With owls who hoot and a raccoon run.
The babbling brook sets the rhythm so sweet,
While crickets provide a pulse to the beat.

Beneath a moon that shines with delight,
Bears start a conga in the pale moonlight.
All creatures unite in a jovial cheer,
A furry fiasco that's hearty and near.

Enchanted Underbrush Lyrics

In the thicket, squirrels play,
Chasing shadows, come what may.
A hedgehog trips on a stray twig,
Laughing frogs join in the gig.

Bumblebees in disco lights,
Jiving flowers, oh what sights!
A rabbit rolling, feeling bold,
Dancing tales that never get old.

Nature's Symphony Above

Birds compose a cheeky tune,
While a raccoon steals the moon.
Leaves clap hands as breezes cheer,
Echoes of mischief everywhere.

Crickets join in with a squeak,
Underneath the trees they peek.
Doves drop notes from up so high,
While owls wink, oh me, oh my!

Whims of the Wandering Breeze

The breeze teases a floppy hat,
Horses neigh, 'What is this spat?'
Swaying branches, giggles loud,
For once, the trees are feeling proud.

A butterfly in polka dots,
Dares the ladybugs to waltz.
Hiccups from the stout old oaks,
As nature cracks the funniest jokes.

The Treetop Overture

High above, chipmunks drum,
To the craziness, we succumb.
A snail races, what a sight,
Losing to a leaf in flight.

With each gnome hiding a grin,
Mushrooms giggle, where to begin?
The forest floor, a laugh parade,
Where secrets and silliness cascade.

Whispers of the Leafy Veil

In a tree where squirrels joke,
A crow wears sunglasses, feeling woke.
Beneath the boughs, whispers cheer,
As ants march on with a festive sneer.

A bumblebee tells puns so sweet,
While ladybugs tap dance on their feet.
The wind just giggles through the leaves,
Like ticklish thoughts that nobody believes.

Frogs croak out their best retort,
While chatting squirrels plan a resort.
Their meetings always full of strife,
Deciding whether chips or ants are life.

Secrets of the Shaded Grove

In the grove where shadows play,
A raccoon pranks in a stylish way.
He steals the berries, laughs out loud,
While owls hoot jokes, feeling proud.

A rabbit paints graffiti, bold,
With carrots colors, bright and gold.
Each tree a canvas, art displayed,
Nature's humor never swayed.

The butterflies gossip, spreading tales,
Of silly deer and their awkward fails.
While mushrooms giggle in a line,
These secret whispers, pure divine.

Echoes from the Woodland Canopy

High above in leafy chambers,
Elves make jokes that twist and wramble.
A gnome with socks across his nose,
Plays peek-a-boo with trees in rows.

Caterpillars hold a fair, so grand,
With every swing, they take a stand.
A snake tells stories of wild bug bites,
Making all the owls giggle nights.

The breeze brings whispers, silly lore,
Of beetles in hats, prancing on the floor.
Each echo vibrant, lost in flight,
As laughter dances with pure delight.

Verses in the Boughs

In the boughs, the branches sway,
A giraffe munches leaves at play.
His neck too long, it trips in glee,
As birds chirp jokes, feeling free.

Squirrels gather for a wild feast,
Where acorns fly and worries cease.
A jester fox plays hide and seek,
With mushrooms giggling, oh so meek.

A wise old owl hoots in rhyme,
Sharing tales of the forest's prime.
With every snap and rustle seen,
Life in the woods is quite the scene.

Poetry in the Petals' Dance

In the garden, petals prance,
Butterflies in a silly trance.
A bumblebee shouts, "Watch me fly!"
While a snail just looks and sighs.

The daisies giggle, so polite,
As dandelions start a fight.
The tulips wear their best attire,
While weeds plot schemes and conspire.

A flower claims, "I'm the best!"
But thorns say, "We're far from stressed!"
In this caper beneath the trees,
Laughter sways upon the breeze.

Vignettes from the Wildwood

A squirrel juggles acorns high,
While a rabbit hops and asks, "Why?"
The trees lean in to eavesdrop near,
Cracking jokes without a fear.

Frogs serenade with ribbits loud,
While crickets form a quirky crowd.
The fox tells tales that twist and turn,
Leaves rustle with giggles in return.

A raccoon plays the tambourine,
Making music, oh so keen!
With each note, the forest grins,
As fireflies dance, and twilight begins.

Nature's Dialogue in the Shade

Under branches, shadows wiggle,
The owls hoot while the squirrels giggle.
A lizard lounges, soaking rays,
As ants march on in silly ways.

The flowers gossip, petals aflutter,
"Did you see that frog? What a stutter!"
The willow tree shakes its leafy head,
"Oh hush, you petals! Time to spread!"

Birds engage in witty banter,
Chickadees chirp, and sparrows canter.
Amidst soft murmurs, nature's play,
Creates a stage where all can sway.

Sonnet of the Sun-dappled Earth

The sun peeks down, with rays so bold,
While shadows dance like stories told.
A caterpillar trips, oh dear!
And laughs are echoed far and near.

A ladybug with polka dots,
In her tiny world, giggles a lot.
Once chased by ants, she took a ride,
On a chocolate chip—what a wild glide!

The breeze whispers jokes on its way,
Ruffling leaves that sway and play.
In nature's theater, all comes alive,
With silly creatures, we laugh and thrive.

Canopies of Chronicles

In a grove where squirrels debate,
A chipmunk claims he's met his fate.
The trees all gossip, laugh and twist,
And mushrooms dance upon the mist.

With owls wearing tiny glasses,
They read the trees' ancient papers.
They chuckle at the dreams we weave,
As moonlight starts to brightly leave.

A breeze now tickles furry tails,
While insects tell their grand old tales.
The acorns giggle, roll and race,
In strange and silly woodland space.

Beneath green leaves, the laughter swells,
Where forest creatures share their spells.
They waltz and prance until they tire,
And dream of nutty treats they desire.

Verses Drifting with the Wind

A breeze comes through with scents so sweet,
A rabbit hopping on his feet.
He trips and tumbles on a leaf,
Then shakes his head in disbelief.

The frogs are crooning songs so loud,
While butterflies flutter, oh so proud.
A caterpillar's voice is low,
He jokes about his slower show.

The trees laugh softly in the breeze,
As squirrels snooze on swaying leaves.
The wind whispers secrets rather sly,
While chattering birds all flutter by.

A gentle giggle rolls through the air,
As funny tales flow everywhere.
Beneath their cloak of leafy grace,
The forest holds a secret place.

The Symphony of the Secluded Glen

In a glen where shadows play,
A rabbit tiptoes on his way.
He trips on roots and gives a squeak,
While ants form lines in search of squeaks.

The flowers hum a silly tune,
As bats take flight beneath the moon.
The crickets chirp in rhythmic beats,
While slugs slide by on slippery streets.

A squirrel juggles acorns round,
While teasing birds that leap and bound.
With every jump, a soft thump rings,
And laughter's echo softly sings.

In hidden corners, giggles sprout,
As trees conspire with playful shouts.
The secret symphony of glee,
Is wrapped in branches, wild and free.

Footsteps in the Forest of Dreams

In the forest where whispers dwell,
A raccoon tells his jokes quite well.
His shadow dances, prances too,
While friendly leaves all join the crew.

A playful breeze starts spinning tales,
Of goofy gnomes and floppy snails.
They race on paths of leaves so green,
And twirl and stomp in merry scene.

With each footstep, the mushrooms sway,
As laughter guides them on their way.
A fox releases silly grins,
While alert squirrels share their sins.

Together in this dreamlike place,
Each step's a joy, a sprightly chase.
For in this forest, joy's the theme,
Where all can frolic, chase, and dream.

Tales of the Woodland Whisper

In the woods, a squirrel pranced,
Chasing shadows, he briefly danced.
A rabbit laughed, with a wiggle of ears,
Said, "Come along, there's nothing to fear!"

A wise old owl wore glasses too round,
Gave advice on how to jump and bound.
With every hop, the bushes would shake,
"Careful now! Don't make a mistake!"

The fox, with a grin, told a tale of old,
How he once tried to catch bees for gold.
Buzzing chased him, a sight to behold,
He ran through the grass, oh so bold!

In nature's heart, the laughter rings,
Animals sharing their silly things.
Join the fun, feel that silly cheer,
Woodland whispers, come listen near!

Biodiversity of the Verse

A frog hopped high, took a mighty leap,
Landed on a lily, straight into sleep.
A fish laughed loudly, splashing with glee,
"Can you swim? Come and follow me!"

Bees in debate over flower choice,
"I like the daisies, they give me poise!"
While a butterfly flitted with grace so light,
Said, "Don't pick flowers, they're all just right!"

A tortoise rapped, slow but so cool,
"You gotta take time, that's the golden rule!"
The rabbits threw carrots up in the air,
Trying to catch them, without a care!

In this wild mix, a party unfolds,
Laughter and chatter, stories retold.
Nature's characters, sing out in cheer,
Join the biodiversity, come gather here!

Rhythms of the Foliage

Leaves rustle softly, a jazzy tune,
Dancing in circles beneath the moon.
A raccoon plays drums on a hollow tree,
"Come and join! Let's have a spree!"

The birds chirp melodies, sweet and bold,
While the flowers sway, dancing in gold.
A hedgehog spun, with a twirl so fine,
"Take my paw, let's form a line!"

In the grass, the ants put on a show,
Parading in lines, all in a row.
With a wink and a nod, the worms sang bass,
They wiggled along, keeping the pace!

When sunlight fades, the music remains,
Echoes of laughter where joy sustains.
Foliage and fun, a true nature's blend,
Join the rhythms, let's all pretend!

The Canopy's Untold Stories

High in the treetops, a parrot spoke,
Joked about squirrels and their nutty yoke.
"Why do they bury? I just can't see,"
A squirrel interrupted, "It's a mystery!"

Mice held a meeting, discussing their cheese,
"I prefer cheddar, it's sure to please!"
Then an owl hooted, in laughter profound,
"You mice are silly, with cheese all around!"

A raccoon then shared his favorite dish,
"I love trash can salsa, oh, it's my wish!"
The trees erupted with giggles and gasps,
Forest tales told in secret, no clasps!

So gather tonight, let stories unfurl,
In nature's lap, let the laughter swirl.
From high to low, the canopy's cheer,
Untold stories, we all hold dear!

Secrets in the Shade of Elders

In the shade where old trees giggle,
Squirrels dance and bumblebees wiggle.
Leaves whisper tales of prankish gnomes,
While shadows hide their secret homes.

Beneath the branches, light does creep,
A rabbit's laugh disturbs the sleep.
Old owls chuckle at the jest,
While crickets tune the evening's rest.

The wise ones chat in silent jest,
Fluffy tails with the very best.
They share their dreams of nuts and seeds,
And swap their thoughts like humble beads.

So come and listen, take a seat,
In this bizarre and leafy retreat.
For in this shade, hilarity blooms,
While nature sings in leafy rooms.

Starlit Whispers in the Thicket

When the stars peek through the leaves,
The raccoons gather, all in sleeves.
They swap their snacks and tell a joke,
While fireflies flash, each tiny poke.

A hedgehog grins, his quills askew,
"Did you hear about the frog who flew?"
Laughter ripples through the dark,
As crickets join in, loving the spark.

Moonbeams paint the laughter bright,
The thicket buzzes with pure delight.
Beneath the sky's vast twinkling hues,
The woodland crew shares silly news.

With every chuckle, echoes sing,
It's wild and funny – what joy they bring.
As shadows dance in moonlit spree,
Nature's comedy, wild and free.

Colloquy with the Canopy Creatures

In the highlands of tangled vines,
A sloth regales with endless lines.
"Why can't you rush if you're so slow?"
A toucan croaks with colors aglow.

A mouse pipes up from its tiny nook,
"Quick wit is found in a wise old book!"
The others nod, they love a laugh,
They gather 'round and share a gaffe.

"What's the best thing about the trees?"
Queries the chubby bumblebee with ease.
The porcupine grins, "There's no traffic jam,
Just the rustle of leaves and a best friend ham!"

So chatter flows on every limb,
In their laughter, joy will brim.
In the canopy, where all unite,
Funny musings chase away the night.

The Ink of Leaves and Light

With ink made from the sap of trees,
A poet crafts lines in the breeze.
"Why did the leaf feel all so blue?"
A dancing breeze whispers, "Who knew?"

A ladybug giggles, fluttering by,
"Just write it down and let it fly!"
The paper rustles, capturing mirth,
A tapestry stitched from the earth.

It scribbles tales of buzzing bees,
And all the laughter carried on leaves.
As sunlight dapples the forest plot,
They pen the secrets that time forgot.

So dance across the emerald sheet,
Let every little bug take a seat.
For in the words where giggles play,
Life blooms bright, come what may!

Shadows of the Evergreen Rhyme

In the woods where the squirrels play,
They chatter loud in a silly way.
A fox wore shoes and danced quite grand,
While the trees just giggled, their branches fanned.

A turtle tried to jog one day,
Wobbling off in a comical sway.
A raccoon laughed from a nearby stump,
Saying, "You'll win the next slothful jump!"

The birds sang tunes in a clumsy tune,
Dancing beneath the bright, laughing moon.
While ants threw parties in a crumb heap,
Encouraging friends to join, not sleep.

In these shadows where chuckles bloom,
Life's a circus, all fun and zoom.
Every creature has a joke to share,
Under the evergreens, we all declare!

Songs of the Twilight Forest

At twilight, the owls hoot their song,
A melody silly, not serious long.
A badger brought berries, spilled them wide,
And giggled while watching the chaos collide.

Frogs in tuxedos leapt with a cheer,
They croaked serenades that could not hear.
A hedgehog rolled by in a comical spin,
Hoping to join in the upbeat din.

The trees wore hats made of leaves and twine,
Whispering secrets, sounding divine.
The forest danced with a rustling sound,
As the stars giggled over the ground.

In this lively land where bizarre is king,
Laughter and joy are the songs we bring.
Under the twilight skies, we sway,
Embracing the mirth that comes out to play!

Lullabies of the Mossy Floor

On the mossy carpet where fairies nap,
A rabbit wore glasses, knitting a cap.
Under moonlight, a fox tried to dream,
But a warbling frog stole his sweet theme.

Each leaf held stories of jokes untold,
Whispers of giggles in the night, so bold.
A worm with a top hat wiggled with flair,
Creating a ruckus without any care.

The owls played cards with the creatures near,
Losing with laughter instead of with fear.
While sloths cheered on, taking it slow,
Playing rock-paper-scissors on the go.

In this world where laughter grows,
Even the crickets would strike silly poses.
With lullabies woven from joy and cheer,
The mossy floor cradles dreams sincere!

Harmonies in the Treetops

In the treetops where the wind holds sway,
Squirrels juggle acorns in a playful fray.
A parrot squawks out a tune so bright,
While juggling raccoons put on a show at night.

The breeze whispers secrets of giggles to share,
As the branches sway, free of every care.
A woodpecker knocks out a beat on a tree,
Making time for the chipmunks who dance with glee.

The stars peek in, taking notes in delight,
As the forest creatures throw a party tonight.
With moonbeams swirling in a wobbly dance,
Everyone leaps in a whimsical prance.

Here in the heights, where the laughter's a feast,
Each note is a treasure, a joy to the least.
In the canopy deep, where hilarity dreams,
The harmonies echo like sunlit beams!

Solace Among the Twigs

In the trees, a squirrel's leap,
A nut's his treasure, secrets keep.
He chatters loud with quite the flair,
While birds above just raise the air.

The robin laughs, a jester true,
In feathers bright of red and blue.
She nudges mates to dance along,
To nature's beat, they sing a song.

A cheeky raccoon joins the fray,
With tiny hands, he wants to play.
He steals a snack, then makes a dash,
Laughter follows, a rascal's splash.

The breeze brings whispers, soft and sweet,
As woodland creatures drum their feet.
Together they form quite the scene,
In this wild stage where laughs convene.

Songbirds' Sweet Discourse

In branches high, the chorus rings,
A harmony of feathered flings.
The finch tells tales of seeds gone wrong,
While starlings gather, join along.

A parrot squawks with jokes so bright,
Of sunlit days and moonlit night.
He mimics frogs, who croak and leap,
While all the woodland friends just peep.

Amidst the tunes, a thrush sways bold,
With stories of great worms of gold.
They all cackle, then take a bow,
A feathered act, oh wow, oh wow!

As the sun sets, they bid goodnight,
Chirping echoes of pure delight.
In trees they dream, with laughter near,
Of dance and song, all hearts sincere.

Echoing in the Green Cathedral

Inside the woods, where echoes play,
Laughter bounces, bright as day.
A hedgehog rolls and trips a bit,
His woodland mates all stop and sit.

The owl's wise smile, a twinkling eye,
He hoots in riddles, oh so spry.
The deer prance lightly, giggling too,
At whispers shared in the morning dew.

The breeze carries jokes up high,
From buzzing bees that hum and fly.
They buzz about the day's young blunders,
While trees shake leaves, in fun-filled thunders.

As twilight falls and shadows loom,
The crickets chirp a merry tune.
Beneath a sky of twinkling stars,
The forest chuckles, near and far.

Murmurs of the Dappled Light

Beneath the shade, the grass does giggle,
As butterflies engage in wiggle.
A bunny hops with such great cheer,
Tickled noses, extra dear.

Frogs croak jokes, a bit of jest,
In tadpole chase, they love the quest.
A lizard sunbaths with a grin,
Dares all to join and feel the spin.

The sunlight dances on the ground,
Painting shadows all around.
The laughter lingers, sweet and light,
In every nook, delight takes flight.

As evening whispers through the trees,
The fireflies wink, a playful tease.
Nature's laughter, soft and bright,
In dappled dreams, we find our light.

Cadence of the Canopied Sky

The squirrel dons a tiny hat,
While singing songs and chasing that.
A parrot joins, with flair and laugh,
Together they dance, what a craft!

A raccoon prances, moonlit bright,
In boots he made from butterfly plight.
He twirls around, without a care,
His friends giggle, in the leafy air.

The owl hoots loudly, thinks he's wise,
While under him, ants organize.
With tiny plans they march ahead,
While the owl snoozes—dreams instead.

Beneath the sky, the leaves applaud,
For all the antics, they nod and trod.
With every chuckle, branches sway,
Nature's humor brightens the day.

Odes to the Flickering Sunlight

A lightbulb bug glows near the tree,
Says, "Who needs lamps? Come dance with me!"
The daisies sway in bright delight,
While sunlight plays, it's quite the sight.

A fox with shades struts down the lane,
Chasing shadows like they're his game.
With flip-flops on, he starts to prance,
In the warm light, let's all romance!

The bumblebees, in funky attire,
Buzz around like they're on fire.
Flitting to tunes that only they hear,
Under the sun, it's all cheer here.

Bright petals giggle, all colors blend,
Joking with butterflies, round every bend.
In a world of laughter, where joy does bloom,
The flickering sunlight shines in every room.

Vibrations Through the Branches

Raccoons in a band, what a sight,
Drumming on logs, with all their might.
Each branches' shake causes a cheer,
The melody travels, ringing near.

A tree swing composed of knotted vines,
Calls all critters to share their designs.
A rabbit hops, shakes his fluffy tail,
While a hedgehog joins, never to fail.

The breeze plays maracas through the air,
As dancers twirl without a care.
The forest floor is a stage so grand,
Full of giggles, all hand in hand.

Under the canopy full of twists,
Nature celebrates, never resists.
With each funny note, a new tale spins,
In these vibrations, laughter begins.

Stanzas of the Hidden Woods

In the hidden woods, there's a chatter,
As frogs compete to see who's fatter.
With jokes and laughs, they croak their lines,
While butterflies build mismatched designs.

The mushrooms grow, wearing silly hats,
They giggle at passing squirrels and cats.
Each wind that whispers brings comic slips,
Tea parties with ants, granting small sips.

The grasshoppers play hopscotch in pairs,
While deer spin in unplanned, wild flares.
The sunlight tumbles, caught in a twist,
Every creature here simply insists.

With laughter echoing through the trees,
Nature reminds us of joy, with ease.
In these woodsy stanzas, forever understood,
Life's funnier moments fill the hidden wood.

The Forest's Secret Songbook

In a tree that sways with glee,
A squirrel sings in perfect key,
With acorn hats and nutty beats,
They dance like stars on forest streets.

When leaves start rapping on the ground,
The rabbits gather all around,
They tap their paws in silly ways,
And laugh like children in the rays.

A bear joins in with silly roars,
While shy little mice sneak out from doors,
They stag and hop, their joy apparent,
In this concert, life is vibrant.

As shadows stretch and dusk arrives,
The fireflies dance and flip like dives,
Each note a giggle, each song a jest,
In this secret world, we're truly blessed.

Verses of the Verdant Vault

Underneath a leafy dome,
A hedgehog finds its rugged home,
With prickly spines and sleepy eyes,
It dreams of cheese beneath the skies.

A parrot yells, 'What's up, my friend?'
While dancing ants begin to trend,
They boogie to the buzzing sound,
As giggles bounce from ground to ground.

Frogs croak jokes upon their logs,
While turtles tell tales to the fogs,
Each twist and turn tells stories grand,
In this rich vault where laughter's planned.

And as the sun begins to set,
With every tune, we won't forget,
The forest's chorus, wild and free,
Where every creature sings with glee.

Songs Spun from Nature's Thread

In the meadow, flowers dance,
They sway and twirl, they take a chance,
With petals bright and colors bold,
They giggle secrets, never told.

A bumblebee with tiny shoes,
Buzzes proudly, sharing news,
While ladybugs in polka spots,
Join in, forgetting all their knots.

The wind strums leaves like banjo strings,
As playful tunes the forest brings,
Each whisper echoes, tones sublime,
In this bright world, we laugh in rhyme.

With moonlight's glow, the night ignites,
Owls hoot jokes in starry nights,
Nature's thread spins fun so grand,
In this wild show, we all hold hands.

Branching Metaphors of the Wilderness

In the woods where squirrels chat,
The trees wear hats, and the owls are fat.
Bark jokes echo in leafy halls,
While bushes gossip behind garden walls.

The rabbits dance in floppy shoes,
While fairies giggle, leaving no clues.
The frogs croak tunes of great delight,
As shadows stretch to steal the night.

Beneath the dome of leafy greens,
Fungi throw parties, they're quite the scenes.
With mushrooms bright and colors bold,
Every creature shares a tale of old.

So if you wander near the glade,
Join the fun, don't be afraid.
For in this world of woodland cheer,
There's laughter loud for all to hear.

Chronicles of the Canopy Life

Oh look, a snail in a tiny race,
Can't keep up with the slowpoke pace.
The birds report that it's quite a sight,
As squirrels and raccoons share a bite.

The gnomes wear hats, a fetching style,
While frogs tell jokes that make you smile.
Bees buzz around with a lively hum,
Sharing tales of where the honey's from.

In this woodsy realm, all's fair game,
Even the shadows get a name!
A quick tickle from a cheeky breeze,
Leaves us all giggling among the trees.

So take a stroll, and join the fun,
Adventure awaits for everyone.
With laughter flowing, you'll soon agree,
The forest whispers secrets, come see!

Dreamlike Dialogues in the Depths

Down here where the shadows frolic about,
Each leaf whispers secrets, there's no doubt.
With rabbits spinning tales of folly,
And crickets chirping a jolly melody.

A caterpillar dons its tiny cape,
As fireflies ignite the dreamy landscape.
Mushrooms giggle, their tops all a-flare,
While hedgehogs delve into their own compare.

Every nook hides a whimsical quirk,
Where nature's lovers merrily lurk.
And up in the treetops, what's that? Oh dear!
A raccoon juggling snacks, what a show here!

So come along, let's paint the air,
With laughter loud, and stories rare.
In this forest, dreams take flight,
With conversation blooming, every night.

Nature's Script Among the Shadows

In the forest, a script takes form,
Where vines twist tales, and wildlings swarm.
Trees giggle softly to each passing breeze,
As shadows dance with the greatest of ease.

A bear playing chess with a wise old dove,
While butterflies flutter, the game they love.
Each leaf turns pages of stories grand,
Woven with laughter across the land.

The flowers debate about colors bright,
While ants relay dramas from morning to night.
Even the rocks join in the cheer,
Bouncing around with jokes that are clear.

So venture forth, enjoy the charade,
In this lively stage, you'll be amazed.
For nature's play never falls flat,
It's a whimsical show, and that's a fact!

Hidden Harmonies of the Timberline.

In the trees, a squirrel sings,
About the joy that springtime brings.
He dances on a branch so fine,
Lost in thoughts of acorn wine.

A rabbit hops with quite the flair,
While ants parade without a care.
They march in lines, a tiny crew,
Debating if they'll bring a stew.

The birds chirp jokes to pass the time,
While nutty pines hum out a rhyme.
A raccoon tries a stand-up act,
But ends up in a snack attack!

In this wood, laughter's truly free,
Nature's jesters, all agree.
With every rustle, giggle sings,
As woodland life does funny things.

Whispers Among the Leaves

Leaves are chatting, all a flutter,
Gossiping about squirrel's clutter.
One says he stole a nut so round,
While rocking out, he lost the sound.

A parrot cracks a pun so bright,
It echoes through the day and night.
"I'm feathered, and I'm wise," he brags,
While showing off his bendy flags.

The shadows giggle, stir and sway,
Tickling roots in a silly play.
They tangle vines with playful grace,
As mushrooms laugh and share the space.

So come and join this leafy spree,
Where whispers hint of jollity.
In nature's hall of playful charm,
Life is fun, and free from harm.

Secrets of the Forest Floor

The ground is home to tricks and thrill,
Where critters plot and weeds stand still.
A hedgehog rolls, a spiky ball,
While mushrooms giggle, standing tall.

Worms collaborate on wiggle moves,
In squirmy patterns, they all groove.
A ladybug spins tales so grand,
As roots confide, a secret band.

The rocks share laughs, a stony crew,
As moss joins in with shades of hue.
The pebbles twirl, they skip and hop,
They cheer for rain that helps them plop.

In this realm of earthy delight,
Funny tales emerge from sight.
With nature's whispers, laughter grows,
See humor sprout as tiny prose.

Echoes in the Emerald Shade

Amidst the trees, a shadow plays,
Tickling trunks in merry ways.
The leaves all clap with subtle flair,
While critters plot their next bold dare.

A sneaky fox in shades of rust,
Creeps by a bush and starts to gust.
His humor's sly, his laughter light,
As he prepares for a jumpy flight.

The sun peeks in, a wink to give,
As dappled light begins to live.
With every twinkle, giggles soar,
In emerald shade, there's humor more.

So join the fun beneath the trees,
Where nature shares its jolly tease.
With every echo in the glade,
A joke unfolds, in light and shade.

Fluid Words on the Forest Breeze

Whispers dance on leaves so green,
Squirrels giggle, a wild scene.
Mushrooms wear hats, oh what a sight,
Chasing shadows feels just right.

Breezes tease the flowers' cheer,
Bees are buzzing, loud and clear.
A rabbit pranks a porcupine,
The woods are full of silly signs.

Trees know secrets of their own,
Telling tales in playful tone.
A lizard slips, but oh so sly,
While dragonflies laugh and fly.

Nature's stand-up, can't resist,
Every nook a humorist.
In this forest, joy's no lie,
Where the giggles never die.

Undergrowth Sonnet: A Tale of Shade

In shadowed depth, the critters laugh,
A raccoon holds a thoughtless gaffe.
Under ferns, they play hide and seek,
While butterflies giggle, not so meek.

A turtle tripped on a rock so grand,
Landing soft in a muddy strand.
With every slip and every fall,
The forest echoes with their call.

Laughter trails behind the trees,
As gophers share their funny tease.
Who knew that nature had such games?
With comical sights, she claims her fame.

In tangled roots, the fun abounds,
With each discovery, joy rebounds.
Underneath the leafy veil,
The creatures' rumble never fails.

Nature's Symphony in Solitude

A lone frog sings a wobbly tune,
With crickets joining, oh what a boon!
The owl hoots, proud in the night,
While fireflies flash, what a delight!

Nuts fall down, with thuds so grand,
Bouncing off rocks, it's quite unplanned.
Squirrels scold the cheeky jays,
In this orchestra of forest plays.

Grasshoppers jump to a lively beat,
While the ants march in tiny feat.
Nature's giggles blend and soar,
With every moment, we want more.

A turtle hums and keeps the time,
The sun sets slowly, oh so sublime.
In solitude, humor takes flight,
As nature plans another night.

The Canopy's Hidden Narratives

Up above, the branches sway,
Where hidden stories love to play.
A monkey tells a cheeky joke,
While clouds drift in, puffing smoke.

Squirrels plot and hatch a plan,
To take a nut from a sleeping man.
With giggles echoing in the air,
Who knew trees had so much flair?

Leaves rustle with a whispered jest,
As beetles dance, they're simply the best.
In the woodland, fun's never tamed,
Where every twist is unashamed.

So join the chorus, big and small,
In this canopy, we'll laugh for all.
In every nook, in every limb,
The humor flows, on a whim.

Phrases Painted in Green

In the woods where giggles soar,
Trees wear laughter, what a score!
Squirrels chat in cheeky tones,
Sharing secrets with the stones.

One tree tried to tell a joke,
But it barked and made us choke!
The leaves all danced, a silly sight,
As fireflies joined the wild delight.

Glistening Thoughts Among the Twigs

Under branches, shiny dreams,
Where sunlight plays in playful beams.
A frog croaks out a witty pun,
While mushrooms laugh, oh what fun!

Twigs engage in gossip spree,
About the squirrel's latest tree!
With every bounce and every jump,
They form a jolly little clump.

Ode to the Quiet Refuge

Here in the shade, let's take a break,
With a picnic spread for squirrel's sake.
Ants march by in a neat parade,
Waving tiny flags they made.

A gentle breeze whispers a tune,
While owls hoot at the glowing moon.
What's that? A raccoon in a hat?
Oh my, could he be a diplomat?

Traces of Light and Lyrics

In a glen where shadows play,
The sun spins tales in a bright array.
Grass tickles toes, a leafy prank,
While dandelions join the prank!

Every fluttering leaf has flair,
A creature hums without a care.
Giggles are heard; oh, where's that door?
To this enchanting forest lore!

Enigma of the Emerald Enclave

In the grove, the trees converse,
They gossip low, could be a curse.
The squirrels giggle, their tails in a swirl,
While mushrooms dance, giving fate a twirl.

A bunny winks, plotting a laugh,
Stealing carrots, what a joke, daft!
The wise old owl hoots in dismay,
'They'll take my dinner, come what may!'

The leaves sway, in playful tease,
While shadows tickle, with gentle breeze.
A raccoon juggles acorns with flair,
'This forest fun, beyond compare!'

Yet whispers echo, a secret delight,
In the emerald shades, mysteries ignite.
So join the frolic, don't be so shy,
For laughter sprouts, where the leaves lie.

Whispers of the Woodland Wonderland

In a glade where sunlight prances,
The fairies laugh, throwing glances.
A hedgehog rolls, not a care in the world,
While dandelions giggle, as seeds are unfurled.

The trees are giggling, branches sway,
Tickling the critters in a playful way.
A deer does ballet, quite out of sync,
While a frog croaks, 'I'm back from the brink!'

A picnic planned with laughter and fun,
But ants invade; who could outrun?
The parsnips join in, they shake their roots,
'Next time, let's bring better fruits!'

As twilight whispers, the stars alight,
The critters gather, all feeling bright.
So chuckle away in this woodland space,
Where giggles grow and joy leaves a trace.

Shade-songs of the Sylvan Realm

In the shade where shadows conspire,
A raccoon twirls, a dance of the fire.
The crickets chirp, a silly tune,
While fireflies glow, like stars in June.

A snail wearing glasses recites a tale,
Of chasing dreams on a tiny trail.
While brambles rustle, in fits of laughter,
The nightingales sing, no worry hereafter.

Fungi frolic, in patterns so strange,
They giggle as mushrooms swap names and range.
A talking tree whispers a pun,
'Get it? Splinters just aren't fun!'

As laughter echoes among the boughs,
Nature's jesters take their bows.
So join the fun in the wooded maze,
Where humor flourishes in myriad ways.

Lurking Verses Among the Foliage

Behind the leaves, mischief abounds,
A parrot squawks, spinning wild sound.
The bushes chuckle, their secrets tight,
Whispered tales bloom into the night.

A mouse with glasses writes down the lore,
Of tigers in jungles who dance and roar.
While firebugs flash, a disco delight,
To the rhythm of nature, with pure delight.

But beware the hedge, it hides chortles long,
Where gnomes strum banjos – oh, what a song!
With beetles tapping, they steal the show,
As laughter and music begin to flow.

So listen close as the moon beams wise,
Within this paradise, hilarity lies.
For among the leaves, joy's always near,
In the whispers of fun, so crystal clear.

Phrases Among the Petals

In a garden bright, with flowers so bold,
A daffodil sneezed, "I'm allergic to gold!"
The roses just giggled, their laughter so sweet,
While tulips did tango with two left feet.

A sunflower chuckled, "My head's in a spin!"
As the breeze told a joke, they all burst in grin.
The daisies then danced, with a fluttering show,
While violets whispered, "We're all in the know!"

A bee flew in next, with a buzz and a glide,
Said, "I'm just here for nectar, not to play pride!"
The petals all nodded, a funny bouquet,
In their floral debate, they laughed all day.

So next time you wander, through flowers so bright,
Remember their jokes in the soft morning light.
For nature has humor, it's plain to see,
Among blossoms and laughter, they all live carefree.

Leafy Serenade Under Stars

The leaves had a concert high up in the trees,
With crickets on strings, they played with such ease.
The stars whispered secrets, a twinkling delight,
While owls hooted rhythms, throughout the night.

A squirrel in shades waved his tiny paw,
As branches all shook with a verdant awe.
The moonlight was grooving, a silver ballet,
While whispering leaves swayed to their own play.

The night was alive, with chuckles and cheer,
As fireflies twinkled, bringing light near.
"Let's party!" cried acorns, "We've got seeds to share!"
As branches clapped hands, none could compare.

So if you should stroll, 'neath the stars shining bright,
Let the leaves serenade you; oh what a sight!
With laughter and music, among trees so grand,
You'll find joy in nature, not just in the land.

Melodies of the Verdant Realm

In a thicket of giggles, the ferns all confide,
With whispers and chuckles, they sway side to side.
The moss hummed a tune, soft and blue like the sky,
While grasshoppers jived, and the caterpillars spry.

A parrot performed, with bright feathers on show,
His jokes were a riot, with punchlines that flow.
As flowers all clapped with their colorful hues,
They sang to the rhythm, the songs of the blues.

A wise old turtle creaked, "I'm quite the slow chap,
But my stories will make you fall into a nap!"
The hedgehogs all chuckled, their spines full of glee,
As crickets played licks, sipping tasty green tea.

So wander the woods, where laughter's the norm,
Where melodies linger, in breezes that swarm.
In this verdant realm, where fun never wanes,
Nature's own concert, it's joy that remains.

Hushed Words of the Understory

In shadows and whispers, the mushrooms convene,
Sharing funny stories that only they glean.
The ferns bowed their heads, with a rustle and cheer,
As vines stretched and yawned, "What's happening here?"

A snail on a leaf took a selfie so slow,
"Watch this!" he exclaimed, "I'm the star of the show!"
The beetles all chuckled, a laid-back brigade,
While spiders in laughter spun webs, unafraid.

The ground was a stage, for wild antics staged,
With flowers as audience, all giggling, engaged.
"Let's put on a skit!" called the wise old toad,
"Just hop in, my friends, let fun load the road!"

So stroll through the understory, soft, hushed, and bright,
With laughs echoing softly through the day and the night.

For nature is funny, if you take the time see,
The whispered delights that make all spirits free.

Songs of the Leafy Arch

Under trees so wide and green,
A squirrel danced, a lively scene.
He forgot his acorn treat,
Now he's got no snack to eat.

The birds were singing loud and bright,
A chorus of pure delight.
But one forgot his tune, oh dear!
And ended up in quite a cheer.

The branches sway in breezy play,
As critters giggle all the way.
With sunlit beams and shadows cast,
They make mischief—such a blast!

A raccoon with a clever grin,
Found a picnic—what a win!
He wore a napkin, donned with flair,
As all the friends began to stare.

Shadows and Verses Intertwined

Beneath the leaves, a dog in dreams,
Chased butterflies, or so it seems.
But rolled in mud with glee and pride,
Now he's a mess, and can't abide.

A turtle tried to rhyme some lines,
But whispered them to ants, like signs.
Yet ants just giggled, specks of fun,
Who knew that rhymes were such a run?

In shadows tall, they play their games,
The creatures boast such silly names.
A frog named Jim and cat named Lou,
With funny hats, they danced—who knew?

Among the leaves, they laughed aloud,
So joyful in their leafy shroud.
With every crack and playful tease,
They found their joy beneath the trees.

The Canopy's Soft Serenade

In the canopy, a breeze does hum,
As chipmunks chatter, oh what fun!
A conga line of bugs parade,
Dancing to nature's tune displayed.

An owl named Fred just snores away,
While buzzing bees prepare to play.
They flit and buzz, a silly show,
Then lost their map, oh no, oh no!

With every rustle, laughter swells,
As stories weave in leafy dwells.
A hedgehog pranced with tiny feet,
His style of dancing can't be beat!

A mischievous breeze lifts a hat,
From a rabbit who sat down flat.
Chasing it down, they laugh and cheer,
In every corner, joy is near.

Nature's Lyrical Embrace

A butterfly wore boots too large,
And tripped right off, oh so bizarre!
With flutters fast, it spun around,
In laughter's hold, it touched the ground.

A frog recited poetry cute,
But croaked instead, a tiny flute.
The ladies laughed, a joyful sound,
For nature's charm was all around.

The trees were swaying, what a sight,
With squirrels hosting a dance at night.
They grinned with nuts as party treats,
In wildest forms and fastest feats.

As night fell softly, stars appeared,
The creatures danced without a fear.
In nature's arms, they sang so sweet,
A funny rhythm, small and fleet.

Soliloquies in the Thicket

In the thicket where thoughts collide,
A squirrel debated with a snail,
"Who shines brighter?" said the furry guide,
The snail replied, "Just check my trail!"

A fox in a tux, quite out of place,
Did a jig on a rock, much to the glee,
The toad croaked back, a grin on his face,
"Just because you dance, doesn't mean you're free!"

The trees whispered secrets, so nearly unsaid,
A bird chimed in, quite pleased and spry,
"Listen close, for wisdom's in your head,
But watch for pine cones! They're nigh to fly!"

With laughter that rustles, the forest alive,
Each creature a poet, each shadow a joke,
In a world where the absurdities thrive,
The punchlines emerge, like a well-timed poke.

Shades of Poetic Twilight

In twilight's glow, the owls commence,
With riddles that tickle the dusky air,
"Who needs a watch when we're such good friends?"
The frogs croaked loud without a care.

The raccoon donned shades, a suave little chap,
With a grin that could light up a darkened night,
"Life's but a stage, with a snack in my lap,
I'm the leading star, and it feels just right!"

The shadows danced, in a merry parade,
A hedgehog twirled with a big, fluffy fox,
"Though we're all odd, let's not be dismayed,
For oddities thrive in this whimsical box!"

As stars peeked through, the world seemed to chuckle,
Each creature a character, making a scene,
With giggles and snickers, like an unending shuffle,
The twilight was ours, in woods evergreen.

The Burbling Brook's Ballad

A brook babbled soft with giggles and glee,
"Why do fish wear such scales?" it mused,
"A secret, my dear, in deep waters we plea,
To look simply fabulous when we're amused!"

A turtle, head bobbing, chimed in from the shore,
"Let's hold a contest for the best belly flop!"
As frogs gathered 'round, it was hard to ignore,
The splash was so loud, it made everyone stop!

The birds in the trees decided to sing,
A chorus of chuckles that flowed like the stream,
They laughed at the splashes, the joy they would bring,
A melody spun from the simplest dream.

So the brook flowed on with a smile on its face,
With every bubble, a giggling sound,
In the forest's heart, we found our own place,
Where laughter and water forever abound.

Fragments of Forest Lore

In the depths of the woods, tales jump to life,
A bear called a meeting, all creatures unite,
"Why does the woodpecker persist in his strife?
That tapping can't be what he thinks is right!"

An owl observed with a wise, twinkling eye,
"Let him have his fun, for it's all in his mind,
We've rhythms and rhymes, oh give it a try,
Just never forget where the snacks you'll find!"

A badger declared, with a flourish and flair,
"Let's dance around stumps, it'll lighten our hearts!
With wild, happy jiggles, we'll jiggle with care,
And scatter the laughter like magical arts!"

So tales intertwine in the leafy domain,
Where humor is plentiful, and joy is the rule,
Each creature a story, in a grand ballet lane,
In the glow of the forest, we all play the fool.

www.ingramcontent.com/pod-product-compliance
Lightning Source LLC
Chambersburg PA
CBHW071844160426
43209CB00003B/405